THE POWER OF INTENT

*Four Powerful Steps That Will
Change Your Life*

COVER

Front cover designed by the author, Patricia Gallant.

THE POWER OF INTENT

*Four Powerful Steps That Will
Change Your Life*

Patricia Gallant

ATHENA PRESS
LONDON

THE POWER OF INTENT
Four Powerful Steps That Will Change Your Life
Copyright © Patricia Gallant 2006

ISBN 1 84401 675 7

First Published 2006 by
ATHENA PRESS
Queen's House, 2 Holly Road
Twickenham TW1 4EG
United Kingdom

Printed for Athena Press

CONTENTS

DEDICATION

I DEDICATE THIS LITTLE BOOK TO LEONARD GALLANT, my beloved husband, teacher and friend. I am for ever grateful that our lives touched, and that we had a little time together. Thank you for everything you gave me: your wisdom; your unconditional love and total acceptance. Your spirit lives on in my heart.

ACKNOWLEDGEMENTS

MY DEEP GRATITUDE AND LOVE TO ALL MY family and friends, who have always loved and accepted me for who I am. Their openness in listening to my thoughts and ideas, their willingness to be on the receiving end when exploring new systems of healing, and the valuable feedback they have given will be for ever appreciated.

A special thank you to Derek Woodhead for all his support and his belief in the message; without his computer skills this booklet would not have come to fruition.

And finally my thanks to Mark Sykes at Athena Press, for his belief in this project and in me.

I wish to acknowledge my unseen teachers, guides and helpers who are for ever present in my life.

TESTIMONIALS

I HAVE ASKED A FEW PEOPLE TO PRACTISE the Four Steps on a regular basis and their comments are as follows:

> 'Patricia Gallant's book, The Power of Intent, is a jewel. In these days, we are easily overwhelmed with information. Patricia Gallant has cut through all that for us. Her four simple tools will, when used, profoundly change daily experience, enhance awareness and empower changes. I cheer for this book's appearance in our world!'
>
> Marilyn Gustin, Ph.D., professional life coach and workshop facilitator, author of A Gate Ajar

> 'I love your book; it truly reflects all that you are. I certainly will use it twice a day and I will encourage my students to use it.
>
> 'Patricia Gallant brings all of her talent, skills and ability together in this book. She has woven her psychotherapy and healing skills all together with finesse and compassion. Patricia

*is truly an amazing woman who has contrib-
uted many gifts to human kind.'*

Merlin Perkins, certified yoga instructor and
wellness coach

*'Patricia is a truly remarkable person, and her
techniques enable us to discover the remarkable
within ourselves, our own in-dwelling divin-
ity.'*

Maria Monks, MA, electromagnetic field
balancing technique teacher/therapist

*'These Four Steps are a healing balm to my
mind after a day in our over-stimulating, chal-
lenging world. I am able to remember the
comforting sense of peace that my original
perfection must be... like a lake that is clear,
deep, and calm. I find that when I do the steps
in the morning, I look forward to my day with
more assurance and loving energy. I recommend these steps to everyone. They are a gift to
share.'*

Deborah Marsteller, MA, psychotherapist

*'Thank you for bringing these beautiful words
and this powerful tool into my life.*

'*The inherent wisdom and simplicity of the Four Steps continues to help me transform old, limiting beliefs, fears and experiences into a trust of my own creative potential and the power of possibility.*

'*Having integrated this tool within myself, I now use the Four Steps when working with individuals, as a therapist and with groups, in workshops and seminars. The profound directive of the words used with conscious breath really helps shift people quickly into a state of self-empowerment and inspiration.*'

Alicia Mary Smith, quantum healing and transformation practitioner/workshop facilitator, creator of *Journeys to Inspire Ltd.*

PREFACE

As a busy design manager for a national UK construction company, I recognise, along with many people these days, a strong connection between lifestyle and health. We feel confident we can become healthier and live longer through body/mind practises like yoga, good nutrition, regular exercise and meditation. As a natural development of this, there is an increasing quest for a deeper understanding of the link between our body/mind and our soul or spirit, which we intuitively believe forms part of our whole being.

To search for our 'soul' is one of the most fascinating and wonderful things we can do. Influenced by the latest research by quantum physicists and cosmologists, our perception of reality is changing and increasingly overlapping with philosophical and religious notions that have existed for centuries.

I believe there is an increasing understanding that we are not human beings on a spiritual journey; instead we are spiritual beings on a human journey.

However, those seeking greater awareness are often confronted with a bewildering variety of books, articles, courses, techniques, religious sects, and so on, covering numerous aspects on the subject. For many of us –as our lives seem to get ever busier and more stressful – it is difficult to find a simple self-help booklet on the subject of using our inner self to assist and guide us.

To answer this need, Patricia Gallant has 'distilled' over forty years of research, knowledge and wisdom into this booklet. Patricia spent twenty years as a psychotherapist exploring and pioneering many alternative and holistic healing methods.

Her booklet provides a powerful and practical method that really works. Through a simple meditative technique, it employs very specific intentions, which have the power to change your life. It gives you a greater responsibility for the welfare of your own body and mind in a way that you may never have experienced before.

For those with strong religious beliefs, this booklet is not intended to detract from any such beliefs; instead, it leads to a greater understanding of our spiritual self and our place in the universe, which can still be celebrated through a religion should we choose.

For greater explanation of this subject, there is a list of recommended reading at the end of this booklet.

Patricia has woven her considerable skills and talent in psychotherapy, holographic repatterning and other healing therapies together into this booklet. If you need to enrich and harmonise your body, mind and soul – read on!

Derek Woodhead

INTRODUCTION

THIS PROCESS IS BASED ON THE PREMISE that all we need to create change is to have a clear intention. When our intention is clear and we believe in all possibilities, then we are open to creating changes in our lives that are for our own highest and best well-being. This gives us the power to reach our full potential.

This simple but powerful system has been created to be used by anyone, without the necessity of having any specific training in the healing arts or meditation techniques. The wording of this process came to me intuitively, as did most of the writing in this little book. The ideas are ancient and have been presented in many different forms by numerous authors.

My intention is to offer this as a powerful and easily memorised Four-Step process; taking only a few minutes it can be used at any time. My colleagues and I have personally found it to be powerful and effective. My wish is that anyone who reads this and uses the process on a regular basis will find it equally as potent and helpful in their own lives.

The process that I am presenting is the culmination of many years of reading, researching and exploring different systems that are available today. Science is now proving the connection, instead of separation, between the physical and non-physical world through the continuing understanding and study of quantum physics. It is said, 'As above, so below.' All of life, in this vast holographic universe, is an energy of light that exists in a duality of waves and particles. This has all been explained succinctly in many books. Some of them are on the Recommended Reading list. I have selected those works that I feel are the most pertinent.

We are each responsible for our own destiny. We all have history, dramas and inherited beliefs that block us from becoming all that we can be. But we do have choices. We can continue to live in the past, blaming our present circumstances on past experiences, or we can live in the *now* and take the risk of creating positive change. I am often reminded of the book *A Child Called It* by Dave Pelzer. From the depths of degradation, he must have had the belief that he could create changes in his life and that he was the only one who could make this happen. So he did.

Living in the world today, we are constantly exposed to high stress levels, environmental pollutants, noise, toxic substances, radiation, violence and wars. It is not easy under this constant stress to arrive at a place of peace and quietness within ourselves. We have to go deep into the countryside to experience the intensity of silence and natural peace. Even there, we can still be disturbed by distant sounds or overhead planes. Many of us also feel uncomfortable if we do not have ready access to radios, TVs, computers, mobile phones, etc. We seem to need to be stimulated by such distractions, to avoid such stillness, to bring us back to the 'comfortable' discomfort of being in chaos.

To maintain the health of our body, mind and spirit we need to nourish ourselves with the right ingredients:

Body

You are *literally* what you eat. A healthy diet with a proper balance of nutrients, protein, carbohydrates and fats is essential to healthy living, as is food free of chemicals, hormones and artificial fertilizers. It is also important to give our body exercise and the right amount of light and sunshine. Virginia Essene writes in *New Cells, New Bodies, New Life*, (1991): 'On the "purely physical" level, are you following what is most loving for your body? Are you eating what feels most right for you at this time? Foods are all thought forms just like our body, and we have the ability to transform any food – with our thought, love, light, intention – to a frequency that is totally beneficial to our body.'

Mind and Spirit

We need a balance between the demands of our daily activities and emotional commitments. It is important for us to allow ourselves time for relaxation, for fulfilling relationships and for acknowledging our hopes and dreams. We need to set aside quiet time, at least twice daily before starting the day and before sleep, in order to reconnect with our spiritual selves. What you think is what you draw towards you, so think positive thoughts. Release negative thoughts by not giving them energy. A method I use is to consciously release the thought and let it become light and return to the source of light.

THE FOUR STEPS

THE FOUR-STEP PROCESS

BEFORE STARTING THE PROCESS IT IS important to 'quiet' your mind using a method that works for you.

One method of preparation could be this progressive relaxation technique: start at the feet and relax all the muscles of the body, ending at the head and third eye, situated in the middle of your forehead between the eyes.

Another suggestion is to visualise opening and balancing the seven chakras, starting at the root chakra and ending with the crown chakra. Or try using deep internal breathing, focusing on each breath, to reach that quiet place within. With each breath, try to ensure that each exhalation lasts about four times longer than each inhalation.

I recommend that the Four Steps be memorised so that you do not interrupt the flow of each step. Also, that you state the words *exactly as they are written* in Steps One and Two, slowly and with meaning; you can say them out loud or silently – whichever feels right for you.

If you find your mind wandering, interrupt the thought; consciously let it go and then continue with the process.

Ideally, start and end your day using the Four Steps – a good time is before rising in the morning and before going to sleep. However, if you find yourself falling asleep before completing the process, then choose a better time for yourself – perhaps earlier in the evening period. If you are awakened by an alarm clock in the mornings, try setting it ten minutes before your usual getting up time. It's a great way to start the day!

Step Three may be used by itself as a tool to centre yourself during the day, particularly when under stress. Used for this purpose, I suggest starting with three deep breaths. You may find that just focusing on three breaths is sufficient to bring yourself back to centre.

To receive the maximum benefit from this process, make a commitment to yourself to practise it regularly. Make it a part of your day to set aside five or ten minutes for yourself in the morning and sometime before sleep at night.

If you wish to understand in greater depth the principles behind the Four Steps, please refer to the extensive reading list at the end of this booklet.

There follows a description of each Step and its purpose.

STEP ONE

'With three breaths, I clear any unconscious self-limitations.'

TAKE THREE DEEP BREATHS, FOCUSING ON each one.

During this initial step, let any outside thoughts that enter your consciousness pass through without making judgment or giving them energy. I suggested the three breaths in order to clear any possible 'reversals' that might interfere with gaining the maximum benefit from the subsequent steps.

Psychological reversals are the unconscious limits we set on ourselves. We may consciously want to make changes in our life, but what we *actually* do is sabotage any progress towards those ends. Some examples are:

❖   Feeling stuck;

❖   Doing things that keep you in a 'no-win' situation;

❖   Putting off doing something that you really want to do;

❖   Never seeming to get what you consciously want;

❖   'Poverty consciousness' thinking, which prevents the flow of abundance.

If we remain in a reversed state, we will continue to limit our progress towards any positive growth. This leaves us with feelings of frustration, anger, worthlessness, depression and low self-esteem. This state may continue for many years and can accumulate over a lifetime, affecting our whole mental, physical and spiritual selves. By clearing any psychological reversals first, we open the doors to all possibilities for change and self-fulfilment.

STEP TWO

(a) 'I now clear my energy fields on every level of all non-harmonious vibrations.'

(b) 'I release past, present and future thought forms and cell memories that prevent me from being who I truly am.'

(c) 'I remember on every level of my spirit, mind and body who I truly am in my original perfection.'

THIS STEP IS THE MOST IMPORTANT IN terms of *intention*. It is the I AM in one's original perfection in being. Through intention you are clearing the energies that prevent you from being who you truly are so that you can remember that perfection.

After each affirmation, take one deep breath, focusing your attention on the breath before proceeding with the next.

An elaboration of (a), (b) and (c) above is as follows:

Emanating from our physical body are invisible fields of energy. The first one, known as the aura, appears rather like a halo surrounding the physical body and has distinct parallels with the body's electro-magnetic force field. All life forms possess an aura.

Extending from the aura are subtle layers of energy, all at fixed distances from the physical body, each one having a different function and frequency. They are closely connected to the chakra system.

Think of the body as a stepping down of energy that manifests itself in the physical form. We comprise pure energy: when our physical form dies we return to the elements of the earth – 'ashes to ashes, dust to dust'. We may unconsciously hold in our energy fields past experiences, memories and thought forms that interfere with creating harmony in our life. For more information on this, please refer to Gerber's *Vibrational Medicine* in the reading list at the end of this booklet.

We hold experiences, memories and inherited beliefs on a cellular level, as well as in our energy fields, so it is equally impor-tant to release any memories on this level, which may prevent you from being who you truly are.

Having cleared and released, you are now allowing a 'remembrance' of who you truly are on every level of your being. This gives you the choices in life without the interference of being that which you are not at your deepest level.

STEP THREE

'I become aware of the universal light surrounding me.'

'I feel this light flowing through me, to every cell in my body.'

'I become one with the light.'

AS YOU GO DEEPER WITHIN, BRING IN THE universal healing light to flow into every part of your being, so that you become that light. Follow the light as you draw it in from the energy fields and feel it from the top of your head down to your toes, penetrating every part of your body to the cellular level. Pause after each statement and give yourself time to feel that deep relaxation, peace and quietness within, on all levels.

In Step Three, you may be flexible with the wording as this is a 'visualisation', so give yourself the freedom to *feel* or *imagine* that universal light rather than stating the words. Once your imagination takes hold, it starts to develop its own reality for you. You may find that the light changes its colour during the visualisation. Stay with the process, enjoy it until you feel that 'oneness' with the light.

This particular Step may easily be used on its own to promote relaxation and as a form of meditation. Use this Step for relieving any physical problem, pain or discomfort. Focus the light over the area you want healed – see the light penetrating and healing the body area – and see it as healthy.

Follow on with Step Four, creating your own affirmations, such as 'I have a healthy — which functions normally' (see page 43 for a list of sample affirmations).

STEP FOUR

'I open my heart to receive the affirmation that is for my highest and best in this present moment.'

LET GO AND FOCUS ON YOUR BREATH UNTIL you feel completion.

After completing Steps One through Three, you may find that your innate being brings to the surface the affirmation or intention that is for your highest and best well-being. I recommend that you leave yourself open to this possibility without pre-arranging your affirmation.

Your innate self knows best!

It is very important that the affirmation be worded in such a way that you are affirming the positive and not the negative. A list of examples follow in a later chapter, but you can create your own intent. For example, if you want more fulfilling relationships in your life, the affirmation might be: 'I draw towards me loving and fulfilling relationships' rather than 'I don't want any more failed relationships.'

State your affirmation only one time, slowly and meaningfully. Now let it go and focus your attention on your inner breath until you feel a completion.

Slowly open your eyes and start your day or keep your eyes closed and have a nice sleep!

SUMMARY OF THE FOUR-STEP PROCESS

Step One

TAKE A COMFORTABLE POSITION, CLOSE your eyes and quiet your mind.

> *'With three breaths, I clear any unconscious self-limitations.'*

Take three deep breaths, focusing on the breath.

Step Two

> *'I now clear my energy fields on every level of all non-harmonious vibrations.'*

> *'I release past, present and future thought forms and cell memories that prevent me from being who I truly am.'*

> *'I remember on every level of my spirit, mind and body who I truly am in my original perfection.'*

Step Three

'I become aware of the universal light surrounding me.'

'I feel this light flowing through me, to every cell in my body.'

'I become one with the light.'

Step Four

'I open my heart to receive the affirmation that is for my highest and best in this present moment.'

Let go and focus on your breath until you feel completion.

SUGGESTED USES

IDEALLY, START AND END YOUR DAY WITH this Four-Step process.

Memorise the Steps so that you can use them any time and anywhere, particularly when under stress. At such times, to centre yourself, just use Steps One to Three.

When using Step Four, your affirmation should always be positive. For example: 'My energy is open and flowing in all areas of my being.' Use your affirmation to draw towards you anything for yourself that is for your highest and best well-being, on the physical, mental or spiritual level.

Step Three may be used to send positive healing energy to any of those dark places in the world that need the light. First, prepare yourself by going through the Four Steps.

Use this process for any physical problem. In Step Three, visualise the light penetrating and healing the body area, and see it as healthy. In Step Four, create an affirmation such as: 'I have a healthy — functioning normally.'

Honour yourself. Be aware and acknowledge subtle shifts that you experience and notice changes as they occur.

A practitioner familiar with 'proxying' can use this system successfully. Before doing so, it is important to use Steps One through Three, or whatever method you are familiar with, to clear yourself. Where such affirmations affect other people they should always be given with a loving motivation and should be for their benefit and well-being.

SAMPLE AFFIRMATIONS

'I live my life in harmony with my spiritual self.'

'I have the energy and clarity to make decisions that are for my highest and best well-being.'

'I draw loving and fulfilling relationships toward me.'

'I am open and ready to receive the mental clarity I need to be successful in —'

'I am now ready to have a restful and peaceful sleep, awakening energised and focused in the morning.'

'My — is healthy and functioning perfectly.'

'I am attuned with the flow of universal abundance.'

'I am at peace.'

'Thank you for the blessings in my life.'

MEANS AND ENDS

There is only one way to achieve any goal you set for yourself.

To achieve inner peace, you think inner peace and act peacefully, moment by moment.

To achieve unconditional love, you think unconditional love and love unconditionally, moment by moment.

To achieve a life that works perfectly, you think perfection and see the perfection in yourself and everyone else, moment by moment.

To experience total abundance in your life, you think and feel the abundance all around you, moment by moment.

The principal is simple: means and ends are always identical.

From Arnold M Patent, *You Can Have It All: The Art of Winning the Money Game and Living a Life of Joy*

RECOMMENDED READING

Becker, R and Selden, G, *The Body Electric: Electromagnetism and the Foundation of Life*, New York, William Morrow and Co. Inc., 1985

Borysenko, J and Borysenko, M, *The Power of the Mind to Heal*, Carson, CA, Hay House, 1994

Braden, G, *Walking Between the Worlds, The Science of Compassion*, Bellevue, WA, Radio Bookstore Press, 1997

— *The Isaiah Effect: Decoding the Lost Science of Prayer and Prophecy*, New York, Three Rivers Press, 2002

Cherniske, S, *The Metabolic Plan*, New York, Ballantine Books, 2003

Chopra, D, *Creating Affluence: Wealth Consciousness in the Field of All Possibilities*, Novato, CA, New World Library, 1993

— *Ageless Body, Timeless Mind*, Novato, CA, New World Library, 1993

— *The Seven Spiritual Laws of Success*, New York, Bantam Press, 1996

— *Quantum Healing: Exploring the Practices of Mind/Body Medicine*, New York, Bantam Press, 1990

Dale, C, *New Chakra Healing*, St Paul, MN, Llewellyn Publications, 1993

Dubrow, P P and LaPierre, D P, *Elegant Empowerment, Evolution of Consciousness*, Norwich, CN, Platinum Publishing House, 2002

Dyer, W W, *The Power of Intention*, New York, Harper Collins, 2004

Emoto, M, *The True Power of Water*, Hillsboro, Oregon, Beyond Words Publishing Inc., 2005

Essene, V, *New Cells, New Bodies, New Life!*, Santa Clara, CA, Spiritual Education Endeavors, 1991

Gerber, R, *Vibrational Medicine for the 21st Century: A Guide to Energy Healing and Spiritual Transformation*, Santa Fe, NM, Bear and Co., 2003

— *Vibrational Medicine: New Choices for Healing Ourselves*, Santa Fe, NM, Bear and Co., 1988

Goldman, C, *Healing Words for the Body, Mind and Spirit: 101 Words to Inspire and Affirm*, New York, Marlowe and Co., 2001

Hay, L, *Inner Wisdom*, Carlsbad, CA, Hay House, 2000

— *You Can Heal Your Life*, Farmingdale, NY, Colman Publishing, 1984

Myss, C, *Anatomy of the Spirit*, New York, Harmony Books, 2000

— *Why People Don't Heal and How They Can*, New York, Harmony Books, 1997

Pearl, E, *The Reconnection: Heal Others; Heal Yourself*, Carlsbad, CA, Hay House, 2001

Pert, C B, *Molecules of Emotion: The Science Behind Mind–Body Emotion*, New York, Scribner, 1997

Solomon, J and Solomon, G, *Harry Oldfield's Invisible Universe*, London, Thorsons, an imprint of Harper Collins, 1998

Talbot, M, *The Holographic Universe*, New York, Harper Collins Publishers Inc., 1991

Tolle, E, *The Power of Now: A Guide to Spiritual Enlightenment*, Novato, CA, New World Library, 1999

Zukav, G, *The Seat of the Soul*, New York, Simon and Schuster Inc., 1990

— and Francis, L, *The Heart of the Soul*, New York, Simon and Schuster Inc., 2001

ABOUT THE
AUTHOR

BORN AND RAISED IN ENGLAND, PATRICIA
Gallant graduated from The Royal London
Hospital School of Nursing and London
University Institute of Education to become
a public health nurse. She then emigrated to
the USA and spent five years in training at
Johns Hopkins Hospital studying to become
a psychotherapist.

Patricia worked as a psychotherapist in
private practise for over twenty years. She
pioneered alternative approaches to therapy
and more recently explored different systems such as holographic repatterning,
neurolink, consegrity and electromagnetic
field balancing technique. As a result of the
investigation and study of numerous techniques for many years, Patricia developed
her own personal method of healing and
treating clients. Finally, in this booklet, she
has recorded a process that can be used by
anyone.

In December 2003, Patricia returned to

live in England and intends to pursue fur-
ther research and writing related to esoteric
and philosophical matters.

Printed in the United Kingdom
by Lightning Source UK Ltd.
116157UKS00001B/86